Goddess in the Groove

Musings from the Goddess Within

Heike Boehnke-Sharp

ISBN 978-0-6151-8082-3

Copyright © 2008 Heike Boehnke-Sharp

All rights reserved. No parts of this publication may be reproduced, stored in a retrieval system, or transmitted, in any form or by any means, electronic, mechanical, photocopying, recording or otherwise, without the prior permission of the publisher.

Please send inquiries to:
Goddess in the Groove
P.O. Box 255024
Sacramento, CA 95865

This book is dedicated to my daughter, my mother, my Oma, and to all the magical women who inspire me in my life.

Contents

Acknowledgment   6

Prologue   9

Virgin, Mama, Witch & Bitch   10

Virgin (Part One)

Justina   13

The Queen & I   16

Freedom of Speech   18

Mean Girls   21

The Emporesses Clothes   23

Mama (Part Two)

Mama, Sascha   26

Goddess Mama   32

Blessing My Way   35

This Morning I Looked in the Mirror   40

Attached Teens, Angels of the Future?   43

The Oasis, Poem   47

My Little Man   48

Witch (Part Three)

Heike   51

Blessed with Two Miracles   59

What Will I Be When I Grow Up?   60

Gypsy Blood, Poem   63

$200 Hat   64
Circle of Power   67
Hairy Armpits   70
Angry Women   72
Passion   76

Bitch (Part Four)
Oma   80
Reborn Goddess   85
SuperWoman USA vs. Mrs. America   88
We Will Miss You, Papa   91
Remember Opa   94

Epilogue   98

About the Author   99

ACKNOWLEDGMENTS

You would not be reading this book right now without the love, support, and prodding of my "tribe". This book is a community effort. The sweat, tears, and laughter of many people are what completed this mission. Tributes and recognition go to so many wonderful people so for the sake of space I will pull out a few. I do this with everyone in my heart.

Thanks to my mother who raised me to have opinions, to stand out, and to stand up for what I believe. Thanks to my Oma who was always strong and dependable and who always tells me how proud she is of my accomplishments. The older I get the more I learn from her. Thanks to my husband, John, who doesn't burst out laughing when I tell him that I just discovered my "it" for the 10th time, and who took the kids on fieldtrips whenever I needed a quiet moment to concentrate on this book.

Thank you to my daughter, Justina, my first born. She was my portal into the circle of Goddesses. She renamed herself "Athena" at three years old, and has been my goddess guide ever since she was born. I must not forget my son, Benjamin, who volunteers his dad for playtime when "mom needs a quiet moment to work on her book".

Last, but not least, are the women who helped me make this book happen. Loana Sparrevahn, my copy editor and master of content. If the story did not either make her laugh or cry in front of her clients at her cafe' it did not make it into the book. Sharon Sturnbull, author of the "Goddess Gift", and web-goddess of the same named website. She is my inspiration and I believe her Goddess Quiz led me by telling me what path I should be taking. Thank you to all my friends who encouraged me by telling me that they will buy my book if it is as good as my articles, and who kept asking me: "So when is it going to be done?". Thanks to Mary Goulet of MomsTown.com, who did some last minute editing.

Here it is, with blessings & thanks.

PROLOGUE

"Because I can."

I don't know the name of the inspirational woman who said, "Because I can", when asked in a magazine article why she wrote such a controversial story. It instantly became my mantra. So, if it was you, I thank you.

Why do I speak out? Because I can. Why did I launch my uncensored website for women? Because I can. Why do I wear crazy clothes and big Goddess pendants? Because I can. Why did I compile this book? Because I CAN!

On every page you will find a piece of me and hopefully recognize a piece of you.

"Goddess in the Groove" is the title of my website that I launched many years ago. I was writing for several online magazines at the time and was told that my articles were "too explicit and not family friendly". I was being censored. I decided to start my own website where I can say what I want. The "Goddess in the Groove" was born.

This book is an extension of my website. It is short, and meant to stir some thoughts. You will find articles from my past which still inspire me or make me laugh to this day. There are also many new musings that have never published before. You will find past, present, and future in the pages of this book.

I dedicate this book to my Oma, my mother, and to my daughter, to the women in my life, to the women I will touch without knowing them, to my husband (Goddess, bless him! You will understand why as you read on), and to my son, who will understand women a little better than other boys because pink is his favorite color and he is all boy.

I have used one of my favorite stories as a thread throughout the book, *Virgin, Mama, Witch, & Bitch*. This is my personal evolution; one that is of course never-ending.

Each section starts with an interview of a dear woman in my life.

Virgin ~ For the girls; the young Goddesses in training, and for the women finding themselves. This is innocent and light reading on the many facets of life.

Mama ~ For the mamas out there in all their diverse glory.

Witch ~ Stories of spirit and healing

Bitch ~ Women who speak out; spiritual crones.

Live freely, laugh deeply.
Blessings,
Heike

Virgin, Mama, Witch & Bitch

When a girl baby is born she is already born into a world of "must be". Women's roles start at this early stage. Girls are supposed to wear pretty dresses and do "girlie" things. Goddess forbid, the little girl child is not "cute" since little girls are supposed to look like little dolls. How many times have you heard: "I wish I had a little girl? I could dress her up and do her hair; they are so fun!" Little girls that play with boy things, or are dirty, rough, and wear pants all the time are considered "tomboys", they are just not considered *real* little girls.

Puberty starts and we are confronted with the term *virgin,* but not in the sense of generations past when being a virgin was a status symbol of high honor. Society has teenage girls believing that it is a disgrace to be a virgin. Their peers and society pressure them into sex too early, telling them it is the thing to do. The one who actually "does it" is the one who ends up a teenage mama. For the lucky girls the virgin represents the stage of beauty and growth. Girls grow breasts, have their first menses, and slowly become women. In many societies and cultures this stage is still honored with beautiful celebrations and rites of passage. We women need to give our girls the knowledge and self-esteem that helps them develop. We have to teach them that *they* have the right to decide over their bodies and their destiny by giving them choices. The *virgin* is a stage of purity and beauty not just a metaphoric term as to whether you have had sex or not.

For most women the next stage is *Mama*. They get married and become a wife and the new mama to their husband, or they perform the miracle of birthing a new human child. Some women choose to skip this stage altogether (though I believe we all have the "Mama" instilled in us and play this role for someone or something in our lives). No matter how well we try to prepare we cannot study for this role, we must grow into it.

Intuition and experience turn us into female masters; nurturers with the goal of protecting our kingdom. We portray this role with fierceness and mamas are often compared to tigresses protecting their cub. The variations of mamas are as diverse as women themselves. Some women stand by their man till death do they part, some women refer to their career or business accomplishment as *their baby,* and others protect and live for their children.

The *Witch* is the spiritual side of a woman. Witches, before their discrimination and elimination, were women of great status and honor. Their rank in society was high and powerful. They were healers; women whose intuition and knowledge let them perform great deeds. They were not always beauties, but their aura of power and self-confidence made them beautiful, no matter what their outer shell portrayed. When today's woman reaches this stage she is ready for change and self-fulfillment. She is ready to find her inner-self and true meaning in life. She begins to turn to meditation, psychics, aromatherapy, yoga, or other forms of natural healing to comfort her inner spirit. In this stage, a woman stops dieting, dying, and otherwise torturing herself to fit into society's *beauty* ideal. She turns her back and looks to her inner beauty. She becomes more confident, starts making changes, and then the *Bitch* emerges.

The *Bitch* is in us as early as the toddler stage, we just don't know it. When we discover her for the first time, we instantly want to suppress her due to "etiquette". But boy, when we need her is she ever helpful! She is our "other self" that comes out when we feel threatened, cheated, or confronted. When we are in a bad place because something in our life is just not right our first step to changing it is to become *bitchy*. Some women get stuck on this step for a very long time but sooner or later they realize it and move forward, using it only when needed.

In corporate America, strong and powerful women are often referred to as "bitches" by their male counterparts or employees of both sexes because that attitude is what keeps them above ground and in charge. People are intimidated and of course annoyed by bitchy women, but if you look at it as a *completing* stage you will see your sisters in a much rosier light!

Take a look at yourself. What stage are you in now? And remember, the next time someone calls you a *Bitch*, you can just smile and say: "Why, thank you!" The circle is becoming complete.

Justina

Justina is my first born.

I will never forget the moment she came into this world and she was laid on my belly. She looked into my eyes as such a wise, little human. Her big, dark brown eyes were so deep; they just looked right into my soul. I had never seen such a beautiful creature in my life.

Since then my baby has blossomed into a little goddess. She has always been extraordinary. Once, at age three we were reading Greek myths and she turned to me and exclaimed, "I am Athena!" Yes, she is. She adopted the name Athena that day and has never looked back.

She changed my life dramatically. All of the sudden, I was a mother of a girl, a beautiful girl. A girl growing up in a society that does not honor the innocence of childhood, a society that markets to little girls as if they were little women. My mission is to make sure she grows up at her own pace, respecting herself and growing strong.

Justina is my inspiration for many things. You will meet my little goddess in my stories, but here she is in her own words, completely uncensored.

What do you think is the difference between being a 10-year old girl today, and when I was a 10-year old girl?
"When you were a girl you had more responsibilities. You were alone at home and had to take care of the whole house. I don't have that kind of responsibility. There was not as much technology and I think girls were not as obsessed with being teenagers. They can't wait to be "old" and cannot enjoy the time they have as children. I think later they will regret it. Most of the magazines and the media geared towards young girls seem to have fashion and boy stuff in them, pressuring young girls to be someone different than they really are. It is hard for me because I love to read, but I am not interested in things like that. "

What do you like about being a girl?
"That is a hard question. I like being a girl because being a girl is being a goddess. I just like being a girl because I am a girl."

What don't you like about being a girl?
"Stereotypes. Cattiness. When I was going to school many girls did the "I am popular, you are not." thing. I wish girls weren't so mean to each other."

What do you want to tell other 10-year old girl's?

"Be who you are no matter what other people tell you. If you be who you are it will reflect on your future."

How can girls empower the world?

"By getting an education, listening, and getting first-hand information about everything they want to know. Never be afraid to ask questions, and ask the right person."

She is innocent and fairylike, yet deep and wise. She makes her mama proud!

The Queen and I

I am used to the fact that my 4 year old daughter is a strong woman disguised in a small body. Yet, she never ceases to amaze me.

One afternoon, we were sitting at the table having a snack when she stated "Momma, I am going to be the Queen of the house today." "Ok" I say. "Good. Now you have to do everything I say." she tells me with her most winning smile. "I see." I said. "Now I have to go dress like a Queen." Off she went, backwards, to her room sporting a perfect "Princess (Queen, of course!) Wave."

When she returns she is wearing an aqua tank top with Scooby Doo™ on the front, white tights (it was 105° that day), a wraparound skirt from a past "Aladdin" ballet recital that fit her 5-months ago, black wedge heel play shoes covered with rhinestones, and to top it off, her rhinestone tiara with pink marabou feathers was perched on her head of wild curls. "My, aren't you a beautiful queen?" I said. She was quite a bright sight.

That evening during dinner my daughter, who was still fully adorned, informed my husband that she had taken over my crown and that she was reigning for the day. After dinner Daddy set off to the grocery store for some dessert and her majesty decided she wanted to go too. Now Daddy is a bit more conservative than I am and I suspiciously asked him, "*you* are taking her like that?" "Yes". Well, there is no arguing with The Queen.

When they returned my husband was still laughing. The Queen was the attraction of the night at the store. I had immediate regrets that I did not secretly follow them with the video camera. He described her pushing her "Shopper in Training" cart through the aisles with head held high (she *can* walk better than Momma in heels) giving anyone who acknowledged her the "Queen Wave" and delegating the items to be bought and placed in her cart. The Kingdom was in awe, someone even took a picture.

My little Queen. Even though Daddy is usually more reluctant to take her out when she dresses herself we are letting her play out her individuality in public. Garish colors and flamboyant costumes are her trademark. We celebrate her individual style, and I hope it continues well into adulthood!

LONG REIGN THE QUEEN!

Freedom of Speech

Being a very "verbal" couple my husband and I always knew we would never have a quiet child. Even though she was behind her little friends when it came to saying "ba ba" and "da da", once she started talking there was no stopping her. Now she is at the tender age of three and I happily hold intense conversations with her, and they are not about cartoons.

With this wonderful talent for gab comes a very extensive vocabulary. I must warn you, not only is my daughter around adults often when we are discussing many topics, but she also watches CNN, Court TV, the Cooking Channel, and some other "non-traditional toddler TV" with me. This is because I can't stand most children's shows and the little time we do spend watching TV together is reserved for the above. I also discuss with her what we see or just things happening in our every day lives. It is almost a ritual for her to come to me at least once a day and say: "Momma, come sit next to me. I want to talk about my feelings." This is her time to vent or to recap her emotions of the day. When she is done, she says: "Now, tell me about your feelings". This is my moment of undivided attention, one I use to tell her about things that bothered me during the day and things that she did exceptionally well. We cuddle and talk then thank each other. Hopefully I can keep this up until she is an adult.

Too much of a good thing? A couple of weeks ago, I went shopping with a friend. She had our two three-year olds in her cart while I was a few feet away. I heard my daughter saying: "Look, that is sexy!" My friend just about died! Red in the face, she yelled to me: "Heike, where does your daughter get these words?" Poor thing, she was truly embarrassed.

Should a three year old not use the word "sexy"? I am sure you say NO! But, in our family it is not a *bad* word, it is one my daughter caught somewhere and asked me about. She wanted to know the meaning and I told her it is when something is very pretty. So she asks her dad: "Papa, isn't Momma sexy?" From then on anything that is pretty, shiny, etc is now *sexy*. We believe that being open equals education.

We also speak about people stealing children and that is why I always want to see her when we are in public places. She knows I carried her in my belly (not the same belly that grumbles when she is hungry) and that I pushed her out. (She identified that the new "birthing" gizmos that are being sold now are not correct.)

She has gone to school and when the teacher asks what she did over the weekend she will tell her that she cleaned out her room to find toys for the kids who don't have any.

We talk about nakedness and that no one touches her butt or "tinkie" (Ok, I did not teach my daughter vagina...yet).

With all that said, I feel adults often underestimate the little brains we are dealing with. We assume because of their age that certain words or thoughts are just "too old" for them to understand, and that we should protect them from being exposed to them. Until *we* feel the time is right. As a parent, I have always challenged my daughter because I know that her little mind feeds on it. Often people will speak to her and say to me: "I can't believe I am having this conversation with a 3-yr old".

So, when we are out and about and my daughter says: "Look Momma, that is sexy!" I proudly smile and say: "Yes, baby, it is!"

Mean Girls

They are in your daughter's life. They are swarming the school playgrounds in little packs of three or more. They are often either spoiled beyond belief, or frightfully neglected. They are the spawn of the cocktail crowd and they love feeling superior and making other girls cry. They rejoice when they "turn" another girl and make her part of their circle of friends, a clone.

They are the Mean Girls and they are getting younger.

We met our first set when my daughter was in first grade. Don't get me wrong, these are not mini versions of what you saw in "Odd Girl Out", or what you remember from Jr. High or High School, this is the full Monty. They go straight for the balls: "If you play with her, you can't be my friend." "I am popular because I am pretty, you are not." "I am the leader of the band." (See Cheetah Girls and Britney Spears)…it went on and on. Thankfully, *my* little goddess was unimpressed by all this, except that she thought they were pretty mean and hideous. She sought her friends elsewhere and played fairy games.

Second grade was kind of the watered down version, because she found some more fairy friends and the young belly-free clan was not very interesting or interested.

Third grade brings a whole new caliber of these little devilish divas, and they are getting back-up from the older girls. My baby, who is now eight years old, is thrown into the world of girlhood in America. And, so am I.

My baby is smart as whip and lets everyone know it and that is not popular. She loves to play, just play, and that is not popular either. She is pretty, ethnic, and the Barbie Jr. is calling her "pouf head". Note here to my daughter; you are bi-racial. Your hair is curly, (little Diana Ross!) you are BEAUTIFUL beyond belief, and I paid about $300 and sat for six hours to get a spiral perm when my hair was long…it looked like yours for 2 days before it got flat again. This is a mild introduction into racial categorization.

When my baby reported the devilish schemes; how the mean girls divvy out spots to sit at during work time and recess and how they form cliques together and just make her little life hell, I wanted to go find them and bite their head off. Then I swore I would pull her out of school for at least 2 years so she can just be a kid.

I let the fire rage for a moment, and then my goddess guide Artemis, the Protector of Mothers & children, hit me over the head with her spear. "Heike", she said "Your first mission is to protect your young and prepare her for the world. Her future will be littered with mean girls. Make her strong."

My path is set. The mission is on. This is dedicated to my baby, Athena.

Bring it on.

The Empresses Clothes

Remember the story of the Emperor, who was coerced by a few thieves to believe his "birthday suit" was a beautiful garment? He even paid them so he could walk around naked.

Now the clothing industry is telling my 7-year old girl that it is not only ok, but that she should strive towards looking like a "hoochie mama". I challenge you to go into any major department store or clothing retailer and find me something appropriate for a girl over a size 4T.

Not only are the clothes revealing and seductive, the quality stinks. You will have to dig deep to get past the polyester and find some cotton.

So here I am with a growing girl and I am disgusted. "Ah" some of you will say, "there are these wonderful European stores online". Yes,

I know. I am addicted and await their sales like a fish on land gasping for water but, how often can I pay $20 for t-shirt that will get stained, torn, and worn just like my $5 T's? I must say, they look much better worn. They have beautiful dresses and clothes in vibrant cotton that last from child to child. It would be a sad sight to see my son having to wear his sisters' dresses just so I get my money's worth!

This hideous movement goes way past me and my daughter. It hit me the other day when I was driving to school to pick her up. I drive by a high school that gets out a few minutes earlier and I usually have to stop at a light there.

I am amazed at the clothes they get to wear to school! I consider myself very open, even a bit provocative, but this is too much. Some of these girls wear clothes so revealing they look like professional street workers. I am sitting there thinking "Where *is* your mama and why is she letting you walk around like that?"

Granted, when I was a teenager I wore things that made my mom's hair stand up. Remember the very tight jeans that you had to lay on a bed to zip? I remember my mom reading me articles on how they cause rashes and hip dyslexia but, I wore them anyway. Or, the jeans jacket made out of scraps (Not really scraps before I got my hands on it. I had integrated two jackets and some jeans into one and added rhinestones and rivets, yippee!) Yes, I was young during the young Madonna era. I even shaved stripes into my hair. So, I do realize that every generation has a trend that makes parents roll their eyes.

My point is, how can a young girl have and gain respect for herself when she is walking around portraying a slut? Pants slung low with underwear (thongs) hanging out, belly out, high heels, shirts cut low, "school girl" skirts that barely cover the butt crack (I am positive a man with a school-girl fetish started that trend!). What really gets me is that they target girls as young as six with these clothes, see girly idols Mary Kate & Ashley, Raven, etc. I no longer let my daughter watch, buy, or otherwise handle anything from the big "D" for that reason.

How do we fight this trend to trashiness?
Easy.
Don't buy it.

Mama

My mother is a special woman. She is the mama I watched in fascination "painting on her eyes" all the while adoring her beauty. A career woman, she always dressed snazzy and always wore high heels. My mama is like Imelda Marcos, a new pair of shoes gracing her feet constantly. I remember closets full of shoes, many of them with tags still on them when my mom gave them away. I inherited her shoe fetish, only mine is boots instead of heels (they run better!).

As a child I adored my mother for her sweetness, beauty, and success. There were times I despised her because I was often alone or because I was always the last one waiting to be picked up. My mama always had to work. I thought she was super cool for giving me so much more responsibility and freedom than any of my friends had, not realizing that she, as a single mom, did not have a choice. We often talk of my parents' marriage now and laugh.

I was four when my parents got married. My mama says she should have heeded the signs preceding the wedding at Town Hall; my dad coming home 2-hours before they were supposed to go to church, tipsy. Me, getting the chickenpox (you can see the spots on the wedding pictures!), my dad's dress uniform missing the entire splendor, the flowers blowing off the wedding car, etc. My mama was sewing all night and did not sleep a wink. When I look at their wedding picture now, they are so young and cute, but the family picture is a hoot! My grandma looks like she is going to crack.

As an adult I began to realize what a fabulous woman my mother really is. When she was young she drove cars to foreign destinations to be able to see the world. She moved to Rimini, Italy and worked at a hotel so she could learn Italian. She did all these exciting things that you would never imagine when you meet her. She is very quiet, not at all like me. She overcame so many obstacles, and she did a man's work for a woman's salary. Her intellect and talent for language made her "red hot" in the industry, but she always ended up being the assistant to a man. With that said, she was able to offer us many luxuries, and from a distance, we really had it made.

My mama is my best friend and ally. If I need business advice, parenting advice, or just need help picking another pair of boots, I call my mama.

Of course I need to share her with you. I asked her some questions, and this is what she has to say. I am going to give you the German version, then the translation, for all you language buffs. Enjoy!

Was ist der Unterschied zwischen „FrauSein" in Deiner Generation, und „FrauSein" heute?

„Frau sein und unabhängig sein ist besser möglich, man muss nicht abhängig sein von dem versorgenden Eheman (und ob er das überhaupt tut!). Es gibt viel mehr Arbeitsmöglichkeiten und Studienmöglichkeiten. Die Männer sind noch nicht richtig in der modernen „Gleichstellung" angekommen und auch nicht in der Arbeitswelt. Das Wort und der Sinn von EMANZIPATION wird nach Bedarf ausgelegt. Ich glaube, Alice Schwarzer hat gesagt: „Emanzipation ist die faule Aussrede fuer Männer, sich schlechte Manieren anzugewoehnen! " Stimmt!"

What is the difference between "womanhood" in your generation, and "womanhood" today?

"Women are more independent. They are not dependent on a husband or man to support them (if he does that!). There are many more opportunities for employment and education possibilities. Most men have not accepted the modern "equalization", especially in the corporate world. The word, and the sense, of emancipation are interpreted as needed; though good and bad. I believe, Alice Schwarzer (one of the most prominent contemporary German feminist and founder and publisher of the German feminist journal EMMA) once said: *Emancipation is an excuse for men to get accustomed to having bad manners*! True!

Wie hat sich „Mutterschaft" verändert?
„Mutter kann man werden, mit oder ohne Ehemann. Heute ist das egal! In meiner Jugendzeit wurde man noch schief angeguckt! Jetzt gibt es viel mehr Wunschkinder!"

How has "Motherhood" changed?
"Anyone can become a mother with or without a husband. Today, this does not matter. When I was young, you were still chastised for being a single mom. Now there are many more "wish children"."

Wenn Du heute 38 wärst, was würdest Du tun?
„Alles nochmal, aber ein bischen schlauer!! Ich würde mich nicht beeinflussen lassen von der Mehrheit. Deinen Vater würde ich zum Arzt und Psychologen schleppen, damit er seine Alpträume verliert."

If you were 38 today, what would you do?
"Everything I did before, but smarter! I would not let the masses influence me. I would make your father go to the doctor and psychologist so that he could deal with his nightmares."

Welchen Rat moechtest Du einer Frau heute geben?
„Lebe!
Finde Dich selbst, Deine innere Ruhe & Zufriedenheit und geniesse jeden Tag, wenn es Dir gut geht. Die Zeit ist endlich und kommt nie zurueck."

What advice do you want to give women today?
"LIVE!
Discover yourself, your inner peace and happiness, and enjoy each and every day when you feel good. Time flies, and never comes back."

Welchen Rat möchstest Du Deiner Enkelin geben, die heute 10 Jahre alt ist?
„DU bist einmalig, und Du musst nicht aussehen wie Barbie oder Britney & Co.,um etwas Besonderes zu sein, Du bist etwas Besonderes. Folge immer Deinem „Bauchgefühl" und lasse Dich nicht beeinflussen, denke für Dich selbst und lasse nicht andere für Dich denken (auch wenn Dir vorgegaukelt wird, dass es „zu Deinem eigenen Wohl" ist, es ist vor allem immer zum Wohl dessen, der Dir das anbietet!!). Sei stolz auf Dich selbst und das, was Dir Deine Eltern beigebracht haben! „

What advice do you want to give your granddaughter, who is 10 today?
"*You* are unique, and you do not have to look like Barbie or Britney & Co. to be special. You *are* special. Always follow your gut instinct

and do not let others influence you. Think for yourself and do not let others make decisions for you (even if they pretend it is what is best for you. It is usually best for those suggesting it). Be proud of yourself and be proud of what your parents are teaching you".

You have just met one of the puzzle pieces that make me the woman that I am today.

Goddess Mama

You, whatever you call yourself: mama, mother, mommy, or mom. You are a Goddess in your daughter's eyes. Even if you are sitting there with flat hair and stained, baggy sweats. To your little girl you are a princess and the most beautiful woman in the world.

This is a big responsibility. This means whatever you portray is what your daughter will see as the "ideal" (at least for the first years of her life.).

I think I can safely say that we all rebel against our mothers at one point in our lives. I know I did. But when I was growing up, I used to love to sit in the bathroom and watch my mom put on her makeup and curl her hair, especially when she put on her "cat-eyes". I thought she was the most beautiful being. In my eyes, she was glamorous, like a movie star.

I say this because you are responsible for passing the traits of strength and compassion on to your child.

For women this can be hard. We often give up our identity and independence when we have children and we are their main caregiver while our partners go out and earn the money. This can make us vulnerable in many ways whether we become financially dependent or depressed because we feel we are losing our grip and get frazzled with the many aspects of motherhood. All this pressure can make us forget whose eyes are watching us.

Take a moment now to think about the role you play in your daughter's life and how important is every move you make and every word you speak.

When I did this, I cried.

I felt like an eel. Sometimes I do say things that are not inspiring to a little goddess. The important thing though, is that you take the time to reflect and realize from this second on, you are a Goddess Mama and you are going make your little girl strong. That is all that matters.

As I said earlier in the book we have to prepare ourselves for this journey. The only way you can teach your daughter respect for *herself* is by respecting *yourself*. If you are in a situation you should not be in, get out. Find a group of women to help you. Find support online. No matter what you have to do, your children, boy or girl, will remember you for the strong woman you are in the end.

I remember one time when my daughter was about three years old, we went to a Friday night reading at a local bookstore. A performer was reading and singing songs with the kids. I used to sing to my daughter and often made up my own words due to lack of knowing the actual song. So the performer is singing a classic, "You are my Sunshine" with the kids. We get past the first verse, and her words don't match the ones my daughter knows. My daughter stands up, puts her hands on her hips, and shouts: "That is wrong! My mama says it is …….!" All the parents cracked up. It made me realize that I am the axis of her world.

So whatever your situation in life, include her. If you work, take her with you a day and show her what you do. If you work from home, include her too. My daughter helps me set up shows, and goes with me everywhere; she is my little shotgun partner. Show her how you are making things happen.

Try to network with the moms of your daughter's friends. You know, we can choose the girls she plays with outside of school. Taking my theory that *we* really form the way our daughter develops, if you meet a little girl you like, it is most likely that you will like her mother. Get together and talk about things that are happening in their lives, and how you can empower them.

Of course I say "daughter" here, only because when I wrote this, I was a mama to a little girl. Since then, I have also become a Goddess Mama to a boy, and he watches me just as much.

He is going to marry me he says, because I am his "mama".

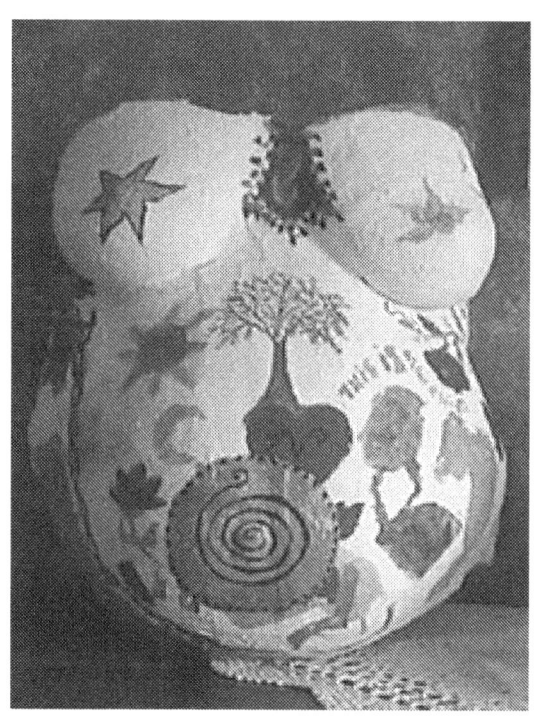

Blessing my Way

When my friend announced her wonderful intention of throwing a baby shower for my second child, I was thankful, but not thrilled. It just did not *feel* right to me, signing up for registries or asking my friends to buy "baby stuff". I still had all of my daughter's essentials, and I would never ask my friends to buy me what I still wanted or needed. As life happens, you find what you are looking for when you need to. It just happens I stumbled on a story of a "Blessingway", and was hooked.

I immediately sent this to my friend. This is how I wanted to pave the way for my new baby and his/her birth. It was the perfect preclusion to the natural birth we were planning, away from all the materialism of a baby shower.

A Blessingway is an ancient Navajo ceremony to celebrate a woman's transition into motherhood. The Navajo have a saying, "whatever happens here on Earth must first be dreamed", and that's exactly what a Blessingway does. It is a ceremony (or the "dream") that is a prelude to a major life event (and, as we all know, motherhood is a pretty life-altering event).

I did stray away from some elements of a traditional Blessingway that I did not feel comfortable with, but chose some of the beautiful rituals as my own. I invited only close friends, and women who had made an impact in my life. My hostess found a Goddess picture to put on the invitation, explained what a Blessingway was and why I invited them to join me. We asked each woman to bring a glass bead to represent each of her children, or one for herself if she did not have any. I also mentioned having a "Belly Surprise" for them (which I will go into later).

One week before the Blessingway my Belly Cast arrived. We lay plastic on the kitchen floor, opened a bottle of wine, and my husband and daughter got to work! We had a blast plastering my belly with the cast gauzes, and two hours later I had a permanent memento of my pregnant belly. This would be the "Belly Surprise" for the evening. I bought beautiful jewel toned paints and lots of brushes, all to be used to embellish my plaster belly.

The evening arrived, and my friend and I had prepared exotic dishes to feast on. We chose not to potluck, as we both enjoy cooking and experimenting. We arranged vegetarian dishes, exotic salsas & spreads, cheeses, salads, and bread. My friend made a delicious strawberry cake, topped with frosting and sunflowers! I lit candles and incense, and put big floor pillows in the living room around the table and fireplace. I laid the dining room table out with newspapers, and put all the paints, paintbrushes, and my awesome plaster belly in the middle.

It was a small group, but full of energy and character. The women ranged in age, with and without children, the children ranging from 3 months to 30 year olds. A few of them were in my home for the first time, but you could feel them coming in and feeling comfortable. Everyone loved it when they saw the Belly Cast and found out they could express their emotions on it while we were waiting for the other women to arrive! As you can see in the picture, it is a beautiful work of art, full of the creativity and love of my friends!

When everyone had arrived, we sat in a circle around the living room, on the furniture and floor. I explained to them why I had chosen them to be a part of my Blessingway, and why this meant so much to me. Then I asked them to take out their glass beads. I had a bead for my daughter, Justina, and strung it on the long string I had prepared. I talked about how she is my angel, my challenge, and how she impacted my life from the moment I became pregnant with her. I passed the string to my friend next to me, and she did the same, stringing on bead for each of her five children. She also told me what she wished for my new baby and me. Each woman had a different story to tell, and we each had tears in our eyes by the time the necklace got back to me. As I write this, I again have tears in my eyes, because I found out things I never knew before on this day. Here were eleven women who did not really know each other, sharing innermost emotions, and I have never felt so close them. I strung the last bead for my baby inside of me, expressing my hopes, expectations, and fears, and thanking them all for being there for me. I told them I would wear this necklace during my labor and birth, to give me strength and confidence. I did and I cannot explain the energy this necklace exudes and how it helped me during my labor. Just knowing these strong women were with me in spirit. This beautiful piece of spirit was then used as a nursing necklace for a long time and is now used as a "sanity saver". Whenever I need to be grounded, I go for my necklace.

After this emotional circle, which lasted almost 2 hours, we were starved! While we feasted on all the delicatessen, I opened the gifts my friends brought me. I received a beautiful leather bound journal, ritual books, sleep balm, a hand knit blanket, and many more unique, thoughtful gifts my friends chose just for me with a purpose.

This was a day I will always remember and cherish. I was in the company of women that I cared for and whom I now consider my sisters. For them, my Blessingway was a deep experience, and they thanked me for letting them be a part of it. My daughter and I made lavender bath salts for each woman as a thank you with a small poem and short note expressing my thoughts to each one. I cannot imagine a more magical way to invite a new baby into this world and honor the woman who is bearing it.

Birthing Helper & Spirit Hand-Holder
Each bead represents one of our children

This Morning I looked in the Mirror
And saw my mother!

What an experience! What a revelation. Maybe it's my 30th birthday coming up? Now, when I look at my daughter who is becoming fiercely independent, I understand my mother more and more! I believe there is nothing like the relationship between a mother and daughter. This special relationship is often one of love and hate and can't be compared to anything else.

This process started shortly after my daughter was born in October, 1997. I was suddenly overcome with this intense feeling of guilt. After a few days I couldn't stand it anymore and under sobs and teary-eyed, I vividly remember calling my mother and asking: "How can you still love me after all the things I have said and done?" My mother just laughed and told me she loved me! My husband said he was proud of me because this breakdown means I finally saw the light!

Do we women have to give birth to a child to understand our parents, mainly our mothers? When I was in puberty I was my mother's worst nightmare come true, though she would never admit it. I came home late, drove a motorcycle, and swore. I picked up new slang and thought it was cool and when it slipped out accidentally in front of my mother she was aghast. At the same time she found me opportunities to work and be a trainee, most of them I visited twice and never again. Did she give up on me? No. When my mother landed a cushy job downtown for a stockbroker guess who she hired as her assistant? Me. I wrote checks, ran errands, posted mail and called my boyfriend in New York. Remember when you wanted to go out but your mother said: "No, because it's raining."? (In my case my transportation was an off-road motorcycle. You cannot drive in Germany until you are 18.) She never told me she didn't want me to go because she was worried and I thought it was so unfair. How many times did I feel misunderstood and patronized? Now I have to call halfway around the world for the advice I used to shrug off. Let that be a lesson learned.

In all those terrible years where my mother surely thought I was not paying attention, I was. I inherited her finesse to make something out of nothing.

I am sure my mother did not realize how she would influence my philosophy of parenting when she cuddled me and rubbed my stomach instead of giving me pills, or when she took me to work. She gave me a lot of responsibility when I was still a young child, since she had to work, and it was just her and I. She confided her problems to me and asked me for advice, when other parents would have said "She's just a kid." My mother always let me make my own decisions and mistakes, even if she had her own opinion about it. We are still very close and cuddle even though I am almost 30.

Now, I have taken on a mother's instinct when it comes to her, a role-reversal. When I call her and she is not where I feel she is supposed to be I leave reprimanding messages. I worry when she is sad or sick. I remind her to go to the doctor and prepare *relax days* when she visits. She often tells me I am doing a great job being a mother to my daughter which means a lot to me.

I am a little sad and teary-eyed when I write this because my best friend lives so far away from me now. Nevertheless, my long-distance company loves me, and I would rather sacrifice something else than to lower my phone bill. Many of us take our parents for granted, until they are unreachable. I am very lucky to have this relationship, but even if yours is not as harmonious, you must forgive and remember the good things you have received.

This story is a tribute to my mother, Sascha, who has made me the insightful and cuddly mother I am today.

Attached Teens - Angels of the Future?
Dec 4, 1999

I often look at my daughter, who just turned two, and ask myself what she will be like when she is twelve? I wonder if she will be independent or if she will follow the crowd. Will she be into sports or will she be a bookworm? Will she want to be popular or will she be a rebel? As much as I anticipate seeing my daughter bloom into an adult, I fear the influences she will be subjected to over the years.

I began analyzing myself; how I grew up and I find myself recognizing the influences of my mother and the other key people who were a part of my upbringing. In my friends and their children, I see how the child's character is formed by the attitude of the parents. Of course, not every outgoing adult is going to have an outgoing child or can you form a child to your specifications; you can only give suggestions while they are forming their little character.

How much of your personality is influence and how much inherited? My daughter has inherited my shoe fetish. She is only two. This is not something that comes in the genes or is it?

We practice our version of *attachment parenting*[1] and I am overjoyed to report that studies have shown "attached" teens are more apt to shy away from the things we parents fear most; drugs, alcohol and sex. Is every attached parent breastfeeding, home schooling, and sacrificing every bit of their adult life to raise their children? No. Attachment parenting is a lifestyle, a conviction, and comes in many variations. I did not know I was attachment parenting until I was asked to write a column in an online parenting magazine.

My favorite way of explaining our version of AP is that we are building a strong relationship with our child that goes way beyond the toddler years. We are building a bond and communication path with our children that will hopefully break the barriers of "I can't stand anything my parents represent" in the future rebellious teen years.

In some of the studies mentioned, attached teens state they feel confident about talking to their parents. This is not because we have lost the role of a parent and have become a buddy, this is because we have built this confidence over the years, in trial and error. Attached teens will not necessarily be the angels of the world, but they can go to their parent to discuss a problem, presumably not as a last resort, but before a rash and harmful decision is made. Or, before peer pressure pushes them into a situation they really don't want to be in. We, as parents, will have the chance to stand behind our children and give them advice, they will make the choice whether to take it or not (I can just see my mother nodding her head in agreement!). Many parents don't have that chance, nor do they consider it, which is sad. I feel for the parents of teens that have gone over the edge, I know they wish they could just have one more chance to talk with their child.

Does this confidence grow because we AP parents tend to explain more to our children and we *expect* more? Or, are they confident because the children are given more responsibility to choose early in life?

I remember many times growing up when I swore my mother just did not want to understand me and that she never went through what I did when she was a teen (was she ever?). That was probably true, as evolving times and a new Millennium will bring our children trials that we can only imagine in our worst fears. The violence our children are faced with today was totally unknown to me, and I grew up in the city. The Cyberage is changing their world; traditional teen recreation has gone from sports and mall watching to cybersurfing and online chatting. Violent video games are getting into the hands of our youngest and are becoming alarmingly status quo. Parents need to be aware and need to accommodate. We need to step back and analyze how we will keep our children close enough to protect them, yet give them enough space to grow and experience.

Then there is AIDS and teenage pregnancy. Children are having sex at young ages and are being infected, or having babies. And still today, you will find parents revolting when a school wants to distribute condoms. I don't understand it. Abstinence is preferred by every parent, and yes, you do not want an innocent child subjected to adult issues, but reality is harsh. Being informed is your best protection, and adult topics and discussions seem to be a staple in AP households.

I have a great teacher yet I have a lot to learn. Power to me and Goddess bless all of us parents!

---

[1] **Attachment parenting**, a phrase coined by pediatrician William Sears,[1] is a parenting philosophy based on the principles of the attachment theory in developmental psychology. According to attachment theory, a strong emotional bond with parents during childhood, also known as a secure attachment, is a precursor of secure, empathic relationships in adulthood.

The Oasis

Outside the lawnmower shrieks,

The leaf blower howls,

The dogs are barking at an unseen fiend.

I hear the phone ring and let the machine answer.

You and I lie on the bed, surrounded by a week's worth of laundry.

Skin to skin, belly on belly.

You are nursing to a steady rhythm,

Oblivious to the noise and world around you.

You and I are nature's perfected machinery.

Your rhythm eases my tensions,

Your warmth and surrender wash away my cares.

I close my eyes and focus on you.

The noise is gone,

And there is only you and I

On our oasis in midst the chaos.

My Little Man

My father and I had a turbulent and strained relationship. Nonetheless, when he called and said he needed my help, I was there. He was detoxing after years of heavy drinking, by himself. He was a wreck. I spent over three weeks nursing to him, reconciling, and enjoying some of the best moments with my dad. One morning I cut his hair, talked about death, and left for a few hours to run errands. That afternoon, he fell out of his kitchen chair and was dead. His body had given up.

Sometime during those three weeks, my husband and I conceived our baby.

This little embryo rocked my world from the beginning. It was a very sad time in my life, and on top of that, I got very sick. I knew this little baby came at this time in my life for a reason. I felt that it was giving me power. I changed my diet, quit smoking immediately, and cut off all my hair. I felt like an Amazon woman and dealt with the pain.

This was my second pregnancy; I decided I wanted a natural birth, and began planning for it. I never gave it a thought that this baby might be a boy. We are a "girl family" on both sides. This baby was Josephine Adriana. If I was not so superstitious I would have had her name printed up already.

The moment of birth came. With my husband supporting me, I let out my last cry, and with excruciating pain and power, my baby slipped into the hands of my midwife. "Oh my God, it's a boy!" is all I hear. A boy? My husband was so excited he could not contain himself and I just held this beautiful boy in my arms and cried.

We all happily adjusted that Josephine had become Benjamin. My daughter, then 4, was a bit disappointed that she did not have a little sister to dress up. He now makes up for that by dressing up with her anyway. My husband gained extra testosterone overnight. This man, who never watched sports and never knew who was playing in the Superbowl, became a sports guru before my son was four weeks old. I just fell deep into his old, wise eyes, and held him tight.

I began contemplating about how "manly" he would be. Will he want to play football, and get hurt? What about girls? I remember the quote I had read in a book; a mother said: "I will cut off my son's toes before I let him go to war." This seemed very sinister to me then but now I understood this woman. I noticed that his energy and play were very different than my daughters'. He was rougher. I never thought I would say it, but he is a "real boy". Will I be able to teach him to be a strong, yet gentle and caring man? I felt from the beginning that this would be my job, not my husband's. One day I heard on a radio show that the mother's role was to be the compassionate, loving entity in a boy's life, and the father was the playful, rough, yet disciplinary one. Am I going against the grain because I feel that all of this is my responsibility?

From the very beginning, my son always had a very calming effect on me. When I was depressed or anxious, just lying on my bed and nursing him would calm me down. As he gets older, he knows just when to lay his little arms around me. He nurtures all three of us, it is almost as if he was here to make sure we slow down, eat, and be happy. On the flip side, he is a wild child. Bruises, bumps, wrestling, climbing, taking flying leaps off the couch....you name it, he's done it. He has given me hundreds of new gray hairs.

Today, when he woke up from deep sleep and called for his mama, I went to him. He just melted in my arms and fell back to sleep. I stroked his hair and wondered how long I could protect him from small and big evils this way? How long will he come to me to soothe him? Will he be too manly at twelve? Before I know it, my baby will be a man.

Here's to all the men who thank their Mama and hoping my son and I will have this bond for life.

Heike

By now you already know much about me.

I am supposed to be rich. I am at the end of my thirties now and grew up as an only child with my pretty much single mom. I did have a dad, but he was not around much, and when I was eleven my parents split for good. My dad was a good man in his heart but the Army (mainly, Vietnam War) made him see and do things I believe he never digested. He dreamed and screamed, and eventually drowned his memories in alcohol. My father always refused the help the military offered him and the help we offered him. Unfortunately, the drinking over the years withered his body, and he collapsed dead right when I got pregnant with my son. I understand my dad better now than I did when he was alive.

With all this, I had a pretty happy childhood. My mom found a wonderful family to take care of me while she worked and traveled and my Tante Erna is special to me to this day. I was raised in city in Germany that I will compare to Brooklyn. It was close to the harbor and the factories, and there were lots of square brownstone apartments (no houses) built in a square with small yards in the middle. These yards were used to hang out clothes, since no one had dryers, and for us kids to be contained and play outside. This is where the working class lived. We also lived with my Oma, who also worked for the harbor, but lived in a brownstone in the city. I love telling my children the "cold butt" winter mermories of living there, but that is a whole other story!

I will spare you all the details of my young life, but it was a blur of activity. I stayed a good kid even though I was home alone often, rode an off-road motorcycle, had a few accidents; I worked at an all- night disco (8p-8a) on weekends at 18, I did not want to go to college, I worked for TransWorldAirlines for almost 6 years and traveled all over the world, I used to eat Top Ramen® and Lucky Charms® (this makes my "organic" body shudder!!), I almost went to New York to go to art school, but my accident kept me home (You can read about that in "Blessed with Two Miracles"). I did a lot of things and made a lot of mistakes. I learned.

I feel that now I am in a stage of understanding. Sometimes, I wish I could turn back the clock ten years, but keep the knowledge I have today. I am excited about the amazing women that are coming into my life every day and how we, as a circle, are making a shift, both personally, and universally. I feel like a "young crone" now.

I answered my own interview questions, with a twist:

What do you want to tell a 20 year old woman?
"Live! Explore! I did a lot of "living" before I had my accident at 21. The accident threw a wrench into my future plans, but all I can say now is that I am thankful that I was able to experience the things I did before my "sabbatical". I am so sad when I see young women throwing themselves into marriage or motherhood without discovering themselves first. Trust me; your body can still make babies after 30....
There are so many things in this world to experience. Take the time and see them, it will make you richer for the rest of your life.

Which brings me to another thing; turning 30 is not gruesome! It is beautiful, and you become wiser. "

How has "motherhood" changed since you had Justina?
"Thankfully, parenting has become instinctual again. When I had Justina ten years ago, mothers were separated between the career mamas and the crunchy mamas. The Mommy Wars. You had to seek out groups to get alternative information. Now, thanks to the Internet and organic foods becoming more mainstream, healthy information just flows. Mothers are becoming more knowledgeable and are asking questions. Women, and companies, are finding ways to make earning money more family friendly."

If you were 25 again today what would you do?
"If I were to wake up 25 years old, I would wish to have the knowledge I have today. I would conquer the world. Now I know what my path is, and what I should be doing. Had I started on this path at 25, I would be settled in my glory right now. I would rethink my

financial planning, since I would know that I would eventually have children. I would travel more and I would learn French."

What advice do you want to give your daughter?
"Stay true to yourself. Cry if you need to. Always come to me for help no matter what you do or what happens. I will always love you more than I can be mad you. I will take care of you first and deal with the issue later."

What advice do you want to give your son?
"Stay true to yourself. Cry if you need to. Always come to me for help no matter what you do or what happens. I will always love you more than I can be mad you. I will take care of you first and deal with the issue later." (No, this is not a typo, it is a ditto!)

Your favorite quote?
"Free your mind and your ass will follow."

I try to remember that life is a journey, and my feet go wherever my brain tells them to go. Your destiny is all yours.

Blessed with two Miracles

Often, people say they have seen a miracle, or have had one in their lifetime. I am blessed with two, and all the wonderful and scary things that come with them.

On May 29th, 1990, two days after my 21st birthday, I was driving my red Mini Cooper to work on the Autobahn (freeway) in Germany. I was a "party girl". I was single, without a care in the world, lived in the city, and worked for the airlines because I loved to travel. I was into sports and started weight training at the tender age of sixteen, so by then I was fit and trained. I was a free spirit, and in the midst of planning to move to New York City to study art. I was healthy, carefree, and happy.

My whole life changed in a split second. I thought I saw a dog running into the road, swerved my car, lost control, hit a ditch, and while my car was flipping around five times, I was thrown out onto the street. When I opened my eyes and realized I was not dead, I knew I had done it now, something terrible had happened.

I was flown to the hospital in an airbed; and though conscious the whole time, I was not aware of what really happened to me. I woke up sore and swollen, still not being able to move, with my mother standing next to my bed looking horrified. I was informed that I had shattered my bottom five vertebrae and that after a 20-hour operation the doctors were unsure as to what my future was. They attempted to collect the pieces of my spine, mend the torn nerve strains, and put it all back in the space that had once been my backbone. They were experimenting, hoping that MAYBE all of this would heal together in a matter of time. To make a long, grueling story shorter, two weeks later another 18-hour operation was performed to put a metal frame around the fragments that used to be my vertebrae. You would have never known what my body was working on under the hospital shirt; I had no cuts, bruises or other marks from the accident. One day the policemen working on the case came in and brought me pictures of my car. I almost threw up. My car was a crumpled heap of metal, a memorial of the moment that would change my life forever.

My only hope was that I had a team of the best orthopedic surgeons by my side. Thinking back, I even considered suicide. As if reading my mind, my emergency room nurse confronted me and told me if I don't pull myself together, I would not even be able to do that for myself!

The pain and antibiotic medicine threw me into wafts of strange dreams. I would dream of my dead grandfather, and he would coach me. In my dream I would explain to him, and to my friends, that I have to rest now because my back was broken. After four weeks I was transferred out of the emergency ward into a normal room, yet still in a "sandwich bed" (two boards that they could clap together, secure, and then rotate to get me off my back for short periods of time). One of the interns brought me a book on Positive Thinking, and I decided to request a "pain pump". This device let me control the amount of painkiller I was injecting. Soon, I was off the medicine, and I could feel my body reacting. I would spend hours listening to "Yellow Moon" by the Neville Brothers on my walkman, letting me relax and daydream of the past and hopefully good times to come. The day I was able to move one of my feet was the day I knew I would make it. I began physical therapy and lightweight training in bed.

I changed mentally. I lost a lot of friends because I was "too deep" and they became so shallow. Even during this dismal time a wonderful event developed, I had a happy reunion with a very close friend. I became good friends with one of the male nurses, telling him what my future plans were BEFORE the accident. He would go home and tell his fiancé', and after 3 months he figured out from my "school stories" that we must have attended the same class. Turns out, she was one of my best friends! We had lost touch over time; gone separate ways and she had no idea what had happened to me. The world is very small!

I had to lay in bed, flat on my back for seven months, then the day came that I was heaved into a sling and a cast was made from my collar bone to my hips (if you know the story of Frida Kahlo, her and I had the same cast.). Even though the doctors warned me that it would take weeks for my system to stabilize, for my legs to work, etc, I was walking within days, ready to go home.

I wore that cast with pride, for eight months, then a brace for close to two years. The metal was removed from my back after four years.

Where a pimple in my face would devastate me in my "first life", I proudly took off my brace and showed off my multiple scars that slashed my body. I even wore a bikini, even though that 2.5 ft scar that sliced the left side of my body and the one on my back were like macabre beauty marks to me. I had conquered. I changed dramatically, from the carefree spirit that I was, to a thoughtful person who believed she was spared for a reason. My mission became to discover and fulfill that reason.

My professor was my angel. He used me as a "display" for his med students; he would put my x-ray on the wall and all the students would analyze my injuries and swear I was paralyzed. He would let them make their prognosis, and then he would point to me sitting on the side, with a smile. He called me the "The little Miracle". But I would never be the same, mentally or physically. I was told I would have to live with pain for the rest of my life, due the damage done to my nerves and spine. I was also told I could never carry a baby, not a big deal to me at that time.

Kitschy as it may sound, I found my soul mate at my hospital bed! We knew each other for a couple years, and could not stand each other. The hours of talking and revelation brought us together, and this man who was always on the go learned patience. He would walk two yards with me, rest, and walk two more. He helped me recover, and stood by me where other men would have failed. He, my *true* friends, and my family watched me grow strong again, and they were my nurturing power.

After many years we finally got married, and shortly before my 28th birthday, I found out that I was pregnant.

I was terrified when I found out about my pregnancy, and so was my family. All we could think about was my back, and I was faced with terrible decisions. I went for my 10-week check-up. I can remember it like it was yesterday, that fierce little heartbeat. It said, "Momma, we are strong!" Right then, I knew this child was meant to be, and that we would beat the odds. I was so overwhelmed with relief, I started bawling!

There were no complications during my pregnancy. I just grew and grew, and as the due date came close, the tension rose. My baby had no intentions of leaving its' nest, so I checked into the hospital and they broke my water. I refused an epidural; I was afraid of losing the feeling in my legs and the affect it would have on my back. I could not take any pain medication, every time they tried to administer it the baby's heart rate dropped. I thought I would die, and finally they let me push. Just when I had given my last, out SHE came, all 9.7lbs of beautiful, healthy baby! We made it! I was in one piece. My back was fine.

I sent my Professor a picture of my little Angel. He sent me a card. All it said was:" A little Miracle, Part 2"

What will I be when I grow up?

"What will I be when I grow up?" This is not a fond childhood memory but a question I am asking myself every day lately, at age 37.

I felt a huge sense of self and purpose when my daughter was born 9 years ago. I felt that my place in the world was to protect her, to guide her and to prepare the world for her presence. I felt my job was to become the "uber mother" and to clear this world of prejudice, since my little brown baby was not only biracial but multicultural. To top it off, I found my place on this earth as a goddess, a witch, and a voice.

When I say I found myself as a witch, it was not that I woke up one morning and found that I could turn the cat into a frog, or get rid of the pesky neighbor. My Oma did not call me and tell me she had a big secret about my family tree. No, I began to recognize my roots. I also found my talent in the study of herbs, remedies, and plants. I see myself more as a "strega", a kitchen witch that heals with her tea and plants. My connection with the earth and my strong bond with trees were explained to me. I began meeting wise women who taught me what was happening with my spirit.

I also found the Goddess. Not being raised in a religious home, I found that the Goddess (in her various forms) embodied what I think a religion should be. In the Goddess tradition, I found the respect for Mother Earth, for the seasons, for the natural rhythm of life, and the respect for the woman in all her stages. The Goddess became me and I became a goddess.

Now both of my children are becoming carriers of the Goddess traditions themselves (yes, my son too). I see that I am their guide, and that they are both strong entities that were born for a specific reason other than just to grace my life with love. They are strong, aware little earth beings.

I can not even remember how old I am. For the last 3 years, I have trouble remembering my age, as if there is some kind of mental block. My writing, once my lifeline and sanity saver, has become rare and sporadic. I am lingering, looking for my purpose, as it has become hazy.

So now I ask the question daily to the Universe:

What will I be when I grow up?

I am sure all this knowledge, pain, experience, conditioning, prepping, etc. happened for a reason. I used to think my life was over at 30 (*don't you love that?*), but now I feel as if I am regressing and am at a standstill, waiting for my call, like I was at 25-ish or so. I wish I could meet someone who would point at me and say: "Heike, you are supposed to be xxx. Now go and do it!" Ah, that would be so helpful. Then I could just start working my way to that goal tomorrow morning right after my wine wears off.

I am a Gemini by birth, and by choice. I flutter. Not only from place to place, from thought to thought, but also from project to project. I see opportunity everywhere, unfortunately, I also get bored very quickly. The curse. I wonder if I will find anything that will fulfill my hunger for challenge longer than through the grand opening. With all this fluttering, I also have the benefit of meeting lots of wonderful women. I have an abundance of great women in my life, and I am ever so grateful for them. I watch them turn nothing into success. While I am waiting for my purpose to evolve I envy them for their stamina and willpower and wish them well. It seems they have their goals mapped out. It is amazing how women can start at any time in their life to reinvent themselves.

That is the beauty of being a woman; you can do what you want once you set your mind to do it.

Hallelujah, sister.

Gypsy Blood

My blood runs hot as the moon turns full.
Deep in my heart I hear the cry,
I crave new surroundings that awe my nature,
the cry of the journey, the adventure's pull.

The family's secret slowly unfolds,
the dark eyes, grandpa's high cheekbones,
the jet dark hair, and eagle stare,
things begin to make sense as I grow old.

I understand now why my restlessness grows,
the ties I make never deep enough to make me cry,
my roots run shallow, ready to dig into new dirt,
the secret stories that only the dead ones know.

Now I know what I must learn and pass on to mine,
I know I must connect to my roots to make them strong,
strong enough to carry me through the shallow parts
of the earth,
Strong enough to take me to the place I belong.

The $200 Hat

Once, many years ago I was making my way through crowds of beautiful and eclectic people at an annual art festival by the river. Out of the corner of my eye, I spotted a hat perched high on a rack. It called me over.

So, I pushed through the crowd until I had my prize in my hand. I put it on, and it fit perfectly. Made for me...or so I thought. The Hatmaker informed me that all her pieces were "uniqums" (yes that was the word), and that this model was for show only, not for sale. I tried to make her change her mind, to no avail. She measured my head,

I made a deposit, and she promised my hat would be finished in 2 weeks.

Mind you, I did not live somewhere where hats are mandatory. Quite frankly, a *poor boy* hat would fit the city and times much better than the hat I picked. It was perfect for the horse races with the Queen of England but on the subway? I did not care, because I *wanted* it and I wanted it *now*.

I received my hat 2 weeks later, paid over $200 for it, wore it out once or twice and then it went into a hatbox where it lived for many years. I even took it with me on my moves. Recently, in the midst of purging and simplifying my closet, I came across the hat. My daughter saw it and was entranced by its velvet softness. "Oh no, you can't play with that" I yelped. Her eyes got big and sad and she went away.

A bit taken back by my reaction I thought to myself: "Now, why won't I let her play with that hat?" Was it sentimental value, or because it cost so much and I still don't understand why I bought it?

In my mode of simplifying and de-cluttering this thought really hit home. How often do I surround myself with items I no longer need or love just because I once paid a lot of money for them or because they may be worth something to someone? When I think about this hat and how I absolutely had to have it at any cost, I recognize that feeling of anticipation in many other situations in my life. There are these totally ridiculous things; when I purchase them it gives me a rush, a feeling of success. Once I have *it*, the rush is gone, the bill comes in, and I am stuck with yet another dust collector.

I have broken that cycle. At this point in my life, it is very easy for me to evaluate an object and decide whether I need it. I am no longer tempted by sales, especially when it comes to clothes (piles and piles of clothes have always been my Karma, and they are the reason for my quest of simplicity and feng shui.), and it makes it easy to *just say no*. I am often donating or giving away things that I ponder on, asking myself *what in the hell was I thinking?* This attitude not only is aiding in making our home more spacious it is also saving us a lot of money!

I no longer give items in our house a monetary value but a "life" value. If it just hangs around and zaps good energy it is a goner. If it has been in our possession for a long time but unused it had better become useful to one of us fast.

Now, to get back to the $200 hat.....it has found good use as the crowning glory of the Queen.

Circle of Power

I was fortunate to be invited to a luncheon hosted in honor of a woman I admire strongly, At this luncheon, I was overwhelmed by *woman power.* Peggy O'Mara, the editor/owner of Mothering Magazine, was the Queen Bee for the day, and all around her was the buzz of the worker bees, the awesome women who are out there just *doing it*!

There were around 30 women at this gathering. We all just mingled, chatted, ate a little, and chatted some more. Then the circle was called and we all found a spot in a big circle of women. We started at one end and each woman introduced herself and mentioned why she was there. Most of us were there because we loved Peggy, but it was interesting to find out how each woman arrived at this point in her life and what they were doing with their talents.

Interestingly enough, for most of us the change came with the birth of our first child. I am not talking about birth itself, which we know is life altering, but *after birth* so to speak. I am speaking of the changes and new found passion each woman found inside of herself after she became a mother. Each one had a very different story and project. As each women spoke you could feel the energy rise and I became completely emotional. By the time it was my turn, all I could say was "me too, same here, that's true." I felt so humble in this circle of power though I knew my role there was one of importance. I am a piece of the puzzle.

I learned that women can move the world. Most of them carry the weight of it on their shoulder's every day. We are strong but our will to defend *ourselves* seems weaker than the venom we spew when defending our children. I found myself contemplating on how to position myself back into the center of my womanhood. In awe I listened to the personal metamorphous of each woman; how she took a challenge that needed to be overcome and turned it into her passion.

I realized that day that there is a hidden mission inside of me clawing to get out. I used to think I was put on the earth to raise my daughter and then my son. I still think my two chose me for this mission but I think my personal agenda is wider than that. I drove home that day knowing that not only was I going to continue being the best mother to my children; but also knowing that I was reclaiming my womanhood. I just wanted to walk around and *GRRR!* at everyone and everything!

That night my dreams were a blur of faces and bursts of color. I woke up the next morning filled with impressions and emotions. It was not until I spoke to a friend that it fell into place. My path was paved long before I experienced the Circle of Power.

I am here to help womanhood to regain power. Not in the feminist sense, but in the earthy, instinctual sense. As I get older, or wiser, I find myself drawn to the Goddess, to folklore, nature, and the power of sisterhood. I am finding new talents and ways to express this growing sense. Women are coming into my life who have already found their core and they are on the same mission as I am. When I recently did a test to determine my "Goddess Archetype", I was baffled to be strongly drawn to Artemis. I secretly hoped it would be Venus. My first reaction was: wrong! Once I started reading the details, I saw myself clearer and stronger and it all started falling into place. I am the protector of the mother and children, and that is becoming my role.

So where do I go with this oversized ego and protective urge? As I said, my path was paved long ago. I believe giving life and identity to the Goddess in the Groove as a website for women, as well as a venue for expression was my first step. I vowed this to be a place for rejuvenation of the spirit, with no censorship, a virtual "Kaffeeklatsch" place, where women congregate. This is also the place where I thrust out my venom, writing is my spear, and my arms are a safety net.

I am on my journey, come join me….

Hairy Armpits

During my weekly evening out with my French girlfriend at a Border's café drinking tea, I asked, "Has anyone ever asked you if all french women have hairy armpits?" She burst out laughing and asked me "What?"

I had to explain. Being a German native with no accent to give me away (only a very German name), I have been asked more than once if it was true "that all German women have hairy legs and armpits". At first, I thought I did not hear the question right, but after the third time I started answering "I don't know, do you want to check mine?"

Although this fits into the same category as all German women should be blond, blue-eyed, and named Hilda, I wonder where the hairy notion comes from. I can picture a geography lesson on Europe "and this little dime-sized country is Germany, land of the Oktoberfest, Lederhosen, Arians, and women with hairy armpits."

To answer any questions, I am not blond, blue-eyed, and yes, I have shaved since I was about 14.

Each European culture and its' fabulous women have a trademark that is world renowned; Spanish women are known to have temperament and the Flamenco in their blood, Italian women are sensuous and stylish like Sophia Loren, Sweden has the Nordic beauties, France has the women of fashion and grace, England has the creative women who start trends, Greece the Goddesses, Portugal the influence of the Brazilian wonders, Holland the cosmolites, and Germany, well, we have the Brunhilde's with hairy armpits.

Hmmm....

Angry women

Women are never supposed to be angry. We are girls; feminine, not brutes.

When a woman blows her top, she is pronounced crazy, hysterical, or otherwise uncontrollable; a menace to society.

It is an age old stigma. Woman are nurturers, we are soft, compassionate, patient. We are supposed to keep our composure, keep it together at all times. We are the empresses of home and family, and both areas need to be cool, calm, and collected. Even as little children, when aggressive play is completely accepted and almost expected for boys, girls who play mildly aggressive are deemed "tomboys". Those that are wilder are probably diagnosed with some behavioral problem. In the old days, women and mothers who "lost it", who had a nervous breakdown or became angry and uncontrollable, were put away. They were admitted to cushy or not so cushy mental institutions, where their anger and spirit where drained out of them with drugs or other torture methods or experiments. These women were torn from their life and families, left in the hands of so-called professionals that were supposed to fix them and spit them back out, perfect and proper. Just like a wild animal that is tamed by breaking their will and spirit, these women of broken will could snap at any moment and become a lethal weapon.

Today, things are not so harsh and sinister, since we have anti-depressants. When I started researching this subject, I was surprised how many women were taking prescribed medication. Many see their anger as a sickness and society accepts it as such. Sadly, medication is a necessary, but temporary fix to calm the waves but when this medication wears off or the body becomes immune, the core of the problem core is not gone.

Sadly, today, as in generations past, there is nowhere for an angry woman to go for support. "Anger" is taboo, especially if you are a mother. The moment you say you become angry you are stamped as an abuser. I have seen it many times. Online support groups, women who became long distance friends and sent each other cyber hugs, will turn like barracudas on a mom who says she flipped out on one of her kids. Once, during a playgroup with women I have known for quit some time, with children ranging from 0 to 12+, I mentioned that the media never concentrates on the "after toddler blues". You never see articles on depression, anger, and post toddler trauma; society expects moms to have their hormones back under control by then. The response was surprising. It was an "aha" moment, you could feel a wave go over these women. Some women initially blurted out things like "You are right! I had depression when X was 3", "Alice started driving me crazy when she was 2, and I thought I would strangle her", "they are driving me nuts!" These comments were almost made jokingly and they stopped there. Nothing deeper, even though I could feel that the need was there to talk more, there was a sudden tension in the group, and the subject was changed.

Of course, the reason I even brought this up was because *I* was suffering from bursts of anger myself and I was disgusted with it. My daughter was five years old, and my son not even one. I was not a hitter but a yeller and most of this anger was directed at my daughter. I was lonely, frustrated, tired, and impatient. I would blow my top for the smallest things and burst out yelling so loud the walls would shake. One day my daughter looked at me so shocked that it was as if someone had slapped me back to reality. Her eyes were so sad and terrified. I broke down and cried. I just held her and cried. I held her so long and hard that she finally wiggled away and even after apologizing to her I felt like a worm. I felt inferior, disgusted, out of control, and just plain sad. Here I had two beautiful, healthy children, and they would see their mother turn into a raging maniac at the drop of a pin. I knew I had to do something immediately.

Where do I turn? My first search was the Internet, where I could search anonymously and undercover. My search turned up almost nothing most support sites were church-based and praised healing through the bible. Though this certainly may work for many women, that was not what I was looking for. I was looking for other women like me and I wanted to know how they conquered this monster. When this turned up nothing I started turning to my friends, but with a veil, since I was too embarrassed to let them know how out of control I felt.

My mother told me to sleep more and though she was right, that did not satisfy me.

Over time I did begin to turn to my friends online, a small, closed group of women that I have known for many years. Here, there was no judgment, only love and support. I began doing yoga, and taking holistic remedies to help me de-stress.

I began receiving calls from women who are still too afraid of judgment to come out of the closet. I was there to listen and give my experience but I believe there is a need for widespread awareness and a need for a publicly advertised place for support.

Hopefully, we will be able to open our minds and our hearts as a society soon so that these wonderful angry women can find their peaceful spirit.

Passion or Mama, can I poop honey?

I wrote the "Passion" article years ago, but it came full circle at a recent dinner discussion (we always eat dinner together at the table. Yes, I know it is prehistoric, but I insist. It is our family roundtable).

Benjamin: "Mama, if I eat pollen, will I poop honey?

Me: No, you cannot make honey.

Benjamin: Why?

Me: Because you are not a bee.

Benjamin: So? Can't I still poop honey if eat pollen from the flowers?

Me: Benjamin, you have seen the bee webs at the market. You know the honey man. Bees go in there and that is how the honey is made. Bees have special honey makers in their body.

Benjamin: If I eat the bee, can I poop honey?

This went around and around for quite some time, I will spare you the details. Once I was done snorting every time I thought about his eager face and innocent question, I began to ask myself at what point in life we begin to no longer believe in ourselves? When do we wake up and lose the belief that we can make anything happen as long as we *want* it to happen?

When do we begin to let other people tell us what is right and wrong and what we can achieve? When do we begin believing that any expert knows better than we do? When do we bury our instinct and drive?

Well, I can tell you that I listened and acted against my better judgment for a few moons but those days are over. I am beginning to find and realize my passions (that is why you are reading this book!), digging deep into my own soul to find what I need. I am realizing what I can *give* now that I am balancing myself.

That brings me to:

PASSION

1.   A powerful emotion, such as love, joy, hatred, or anger.
2.   a.   Ardent love.
       b.   Strong sexual desire; lust.
       c.   The object of such love or desire.
3.   a.   Boundless enthusiasm: *His skills as a player don't quite match his passion for the game.*
       b.   The object of such enthusiasm: *Soccer is her passion.*

Passion is a fickle thing, often associated with love and sex life's passion takes a background role. What is your passion? The thing that makes you feel complete, that gives you a sense of fulfillment and accomplishment?

Being passionate about something can make you come across as strong and focused or insane! Passion can make you lose all sense of manners and conformity. You see your goal, you can smell it! Your dream at arm's reach and are going to do whatever it takes to get there, damn what others think.

I have spent countless hours, days, and years of my life doing what I *should* be doing. I held several jobs and made good money but I was never really happy. I was good at what I did and just stayed there because it was what I *should* be doing. When my daughter was born a new flame flared inside of me and a passion was born; my daughter.

When she was two I stopped working. Remember, she was my new passion, and I was going to do what it took to stay home with her. I started a home business and built it into a stable income earner while fulfilling my need to be with my daughter. I also found my role in speaking out for women, and girls. I became a voice. You would think I was happy and I was for a couple of years.

Again, passion is a fickle thing and it flips on you. One day, while planting my tomato plants I knew my passion for my business had died. At the same moment that I realized this I made the immediate decision to quit. After almost a year of contemplating this decision in the past, it only took me a second to know I was on my way out. As I stepped out of my garden it was as if someone had lifted a huge weight off my shoulders.

When I announced my decision to my family and friends they were shocked and curious. What the hell was I going to do now? Was I insane? I wanted to direct all my energy to a place I had a passion for, the Goddess in the Groove. This is where my head and heart are. This is where I express myself and state my opinions, this is where I reach other women, secure new bonds and long lasting friendships. This is where I laugh and cry.

It has been quite a few years since I planted those tomatoes! Now I know that split decision to follow my true calling was meant to come exactly at that moment. A few days before or months later, I would have pushed it away again. Fear and being comfortable can make it hard to hear your true calling.

When you are at the point in your life when only your passion will make you happy and complete, you have to be able to let go. Let go of security, let go of self doubt, let go of conformity, let go of negative baggage, let go of anything and everything that is hanging on your shirt tails telling you "No, don't do it!".

What? You don't know what your passion is? Then it is not your time, it will come to you when you are ready.

Be blessed, live free, love life.

Oma

This spot was reserved for an interview with my Oma (grandmother), discussing womanhood today and how it has changed since she was a young woman raising a family.

Unfortunately, my Oma, who is 89 years old, just happened to start a prolonged bout with sickness and emergency visits to the hospital when we started to talk. I have decided to interview her when she is up and running again, and will post the interview on my website: www.goddessinthegroove.com. You won't want to miss it.

Even though I was never able to finish the official interview with her I have decided to share some of her story here. Many hours on the phone, long distance, have made me better understand the woman my Oma is, and how her experiences have influenced me.

My Oma was one of two children; she had a twin brother. She was born in Munich, Germany in 1918. When she was only 11 years old, her mother died. She was left to become the "woman of the house". I can't even imagine a young girl, one year older than my daughter, running a household and feeding two other people. Soon, her father was not able to support the two children and her odyssey began.

"No matter where we were sent, I always knew we were not really wanted."

This statement sticks in my head. It was the beginning of her story which she told me when I was 36.

She told me how she and her brother were sent to live with one distant relative or another. These were meager times and the children knew they were a burden to each family they stayed with. They were passed around like this until their adult years.

My Oma always felt responsible for her brother, but when she met my Opa at the tender age of 16 she fell head over heels in love. After a short courtship they married, in 1939.

This is where the story fast forwards to me. You see, when I was young I seemed to be the only one with three grandmothers. By the time I was born my Oma and Opa had long divorced and my Opa had remarried. I only knew my Oma as a single woman.

My Oma always had high expectations of my mother and was not too happy when my mother chose to marry my father when I was four years old. I vividly remember my Oma telling me the only good thing that came from this union was me. With my mom being single until I was 4 we lived with my Oma. I have fond memories of living in that old brownstone with the courtyard in the middle, but one thing that sticks is that my Oma always seemed very strict and disciplined. No one dare wash their hands or put a dish in the kitchen sink after my Oma polished it! That steel sink looked like it was brand new after 30 years!

Even though I often rebelled against my Oma's ways I knew she loved me. She often told me how proud she was of me. I think she was always amazed that the product of what she saw as a failed union between my mom and dad could bring her so much joy.

From 1949 on, my Oma lived alone, and took care of herself. I was intrigued by my Oma's keen sense of money and budgeting. Where I would have called her "stingy" as a young duckling, now I call her thrifty. We used to tease her for ironing out gift wrap with her hands, and folding it back up to be reused. I do this all the time and often think back to Oma and smile. Or, she would take me into the city for lunch at the Hafenamt where she retired from. This was the government harbor office and part of the retirement package was that you would get food stamps to eat in their cafeteria for a nominal amount of money. Whenever we walked downtown to go shopping we ate at the Hafenamt, cafeteria food. I always complained. As a child this food was not as good as home-cooked, and all the people seemed prehistoric to me. I know now that this was Oma's way of taking me out and showing me off to her friends.

If you ever needed money for something big or an emergency expense you went to Oma. I still have not quite figured out how she managed to amass her money but she was always able give. Of course, only after you laid out a detailed business plan. Where was the money going? Why? How are you going to pay it back? Though, honestly, I don't think she expected you to pay it back. She was making a point.

In the last few years, I have spent lots of time picking my Oma's brain. Her life experience helps me make decisions. She always asks if I am happy, as me, as a mom, and a wife. One day she told me, "When I think back, I believe I married too early. We were carted around so much as kids, I got married because I wanted to "belong" somewhere. I wanted to belong and be loved".

This statement was so profound and all of a sudden I understood my Oma much better. I understood why she seemed bitter and harsh to many people and how her strong front kept her going. It kept her from being vulnerable again and from getting her feelings hurt. I don't even know if her children, my mom and my uncle, know how sensitive my Oma really is.

Apart from wanting to hug my Oma through the phone I swore to myself that my children would always feel loved. How many women and men throw themselves into relationships they should not be in only because they are looking for love and a sense of belonging?

Today, I see so much of my Oma in myself. I see her strength, and her keen sense of business and mental organization. I would love to say that I inherited her practical organization genes or those that possessed her to keep everything spotlessly clean, but I did not. I received the opposite gene. My Oma is an eloquent public speaker and still writes wonderful speeches and poems to this day. She watches me progress through life and knows she taught me well.

Dankeschön, Oma. I look forward to telling your story in your own words soon.....

Reborn Goddess

A good friend once told me if you want to keep peace you do not talk about religion or politics. I love to talk about both as much as possible. With this in mind only read on if you are open-minded and can digest other opinions than what yours may be.

At a recent woman's gathering one of my favorite subjects came up: Religion. Now, I don't know if we Europeans are raised with a discussion gene or if we just love to analyze and discuss to the core; but we tend not to take the opinions of others personal. We discuss, take it in, voice our opinions, and move on with our lives, even when it comes to religion.

I believe the discussion started about the intolerance of some religions to the beliefs of others (I will take the names and the religion stated to the grave). I voiced my opinion that that is exactly the reason I do not attend a traditional church as well as my other beefs I have with these institutions. Well, I *believe* I challenged a woman who introduced herself like this:

" I am a reborn Christian and my religion is my life. God wanted us to be Christians."

Really? Did he tell you that? What was your name? And what in the world is a reborn Christian? I have honestly always wanted someone to explain that to me without biting my head off or trying to "save" me. Do you wake up one day in a slum life and say: "I am going to be a Christian today, and all my sins and sorrows of the past are behind me?" A new you, like a baby that was just born onto this earth innocently? Or are you repenting, replacing past sins and mistakes with good faith, thus, erasing them forever?

This lady must have been the mother who told her child that only Christians go to heaven and her child must be in the same class at school as my daughter. This same child must have been taught that it is okay to harass other children at recess and tell them they will go to hell because they are not Christians. Damn all the other religions out there. I was quite shocked at how young the savers are and try to remind myself that my children take our earth saving religion very serious themselves. I still say that to each his own. I respect those that see their religion as their savior, but please also respect those of us that are not in your world.

After this short discussion that was finished behind my back after I left the gathering (I left my little bug on the wall and heard every word), I went away with an enlightening insight. Until this day I was getting pretty frustrated with the constant inundating of my life with religion. The many emails with "God bless you" in the signature and the many bible verse excerpts in business correspondence, etc. Whenever I mention that this bothers me I get blasted and titled a "hater". I am getting tired of people "blessing" me constantly on such a superficial level. For one, I am very selective with whom I want to bless. Last week at the market the organic egg farmer said "God Bless You!" to me after an animated and heartfelt conversation with him and passersby. This was true, and authentic, and I accepted this blessing very thankfully. Note to all, religion is becoming very trendy.

I left this discussion with the knowledge that from this day on, I will be a reborn Goddess. Yes, I am! I claimed the Goddess years ago when I became a new mom. I claimed her because I knew I wanted to save and respect the earth. I knew that I wanted to teach my little female human to respect herself and be strong. I found the goddess/wiccan/pagan/Buddhist religion and knew that each had a piece in it to complete the puzzle of the whole me. They also teach compassion for those that can't see past themselves. I cleansed myself from all my past sorrows, repented my earthly sins, and became a reborn goddess.

Goddess bless you.

SuperWoman USA vs. Mrs. America

Tonight I watched some of the Mrs. America Pageant. Mrs. Indiana took the crown looking like she just stepped out from a gala in her beautiful gala dress and was congratulated by her husband, Dr. Chad. Though I am sure these women deserve the cars and frilly prizes they receive, what got me was the phrase that was reiterated during the show and once more in the finale: "These women represent the married women all around the Nation." Not on my planet!

While we were watching my daughter asked, "Momma, can you go there?" (Beauty lies in the eye of the beholder. My daughter thinks I am the most beautiful momma even with my short, spiky hair, pregnant belly, in my big old sweats and tank top!). I snickered, "Oh, sure!" Then I thought to myself: "When will there be a pageant for the *real* women of America?" I would name it "Superwoman USA". It would defy all the unrealistic and unnatural role models we show our daughters from the smallest "Baby Miss" pageant on and would honor the women who work unglamorous 9-6 jobs alongside their husbands, the SAHM's (stay at home moms), the WAHM's (work at home moms), and single women.

Talents would include: a) occupying and cradling 1-3 kids on average while managing an at home business on the computer and phone. b) Looking like 1 million bucks on a $10 budget. c) Fixing your own car. d) Surviving the Barbie Syndrome. e) Supporting a husband through med school, law school, business venture, etc, and still building a financial cushion for yourself. f) Vacationing as a single woman. g) Teaching children not to be materialistic and unrealistic in a materialistic and unrealistic society…the list goes on. Best of all: Aging naturally and with grace.

Beauty is a big aspect in these pageants; more than talent. I have yet to see a talented and accomplished woman without perfect teeth, perfect hair, and under a size 10 at a Mrs. America competition. Of course all of these women were beautiful but, they were also "uniform". Where are the different colors, shapes, and sizes of America's married women? They have been singled out during preceding pageants. Until 51 women who look pretty much alike, except for their hair color, represent the 50 states and District of Columbia.

I must say, in their recent mission statement the Mrs. America pageant states, "The mission of the Mrs. America Act Now Alliance is to educate and empower America's women to take all the necessary steps to maintain healthy bones as the foundation for securing their outer beauty and their active roles in life. In each of America's 50 States and the District of Columbia, we will unleash Mrs. America delegates as Fracture Fighters - messengers pledged to talk to their mothers, aunts, grandmothers and America's at-risk women about how to create more fracture-resistant bones now." For the complete mission statement, and view details of the pageant, see their official website. It is an important mission, and a good cause. Hopefully, it will reach the women it is targeted towards.

Mrs. America will go on to Las Vegas to represent The United States of America in the "Mrs. World" pageant. I say, next time we send "Superwoman USA".

We will miss you Papa

In Memory of my Father
Hans U. Boehnke
1/31/1939 - 4/29/2001

Though my father passed away rather unexpectedly, I had spent the last 3 weeks taking care of him; talking, planning, and thinking of myself growing old.

In these days, I would often look at my father with different eyes. I was looking at him as a mother, wondering if I would be like him in years to come, and if my daughter would be there for me. We spent many hours talking and all the trials and tribulations of the past were forgotten. I took care of him and his granddaughter was by his side, with the patience of an angel. I do have to chuckle thinking about the two of them on the bed, with Barney & Friends yodeling on the T.V. My father gave me a look of despair but endured it because he cherished that my daughter was by his side.

His death took me by surprise but I have peace. You see, I am writing this as a warning to all of you that have cut your parents from your life. Many of us swear we will do everything better than our parents did and many times I hear of irreconcilable differences. There are things we feel we can never forgive.

I had many differences with my father, and he also did things I can never forgive. When he called me and asked for my help, I knew it took all his courage to pick up the phone. My hate and anger were replaced by fear, love, and respect for his fight for survival. I almost became like a mother to him, taking over and teaching. Even my husband, who had been treated badly by my father, put this entirely aside and helped him without a second thought. During this whole time my father thanked us constantly, because he deep down he knew he was wrong in the past and he was thankful that our love for him was stronger than hate.

I spent the days after his death thinking about our life. Of course, all the mean and hateful things I said and thoughts that crossed my mind but I especially cherish some of the special things. My father spent days looking for blood donors for me when I had a near fatal car accident in 1990, and because we both have a rare blood type, my surgery was delayed until they could store enough blood to perform it. I remember our daughter/father dance at my wedding and his short but sweet "Papa, love you baby" on my wedding picture. Everyone tells me he couldn't talk enough of my daughter, he was so proud of his grand baby that all the neighbors basically "heard" her grow.

Now, I wish I would have stayed a little longer that afternoon when he passed away. What I would give for just a few more minutes to talk. That morning I was still joking around with him, cutting his hair on the back porch, and now I have to comfort myself with those memories. Today, I am thankful for the time I had with him.

If you are lucky enough to still have your parents, take a moment today to let them know you love them, it may be your last chance.

We will miss you, Papa.

"Remember the day Opa died?"

A Toddler dealing with Death

When my father passed away, I was not only faced with death and that my father was now "gone" forever, I also had to explain this fact to my three-and-a-half year old.

The weeks prior to my father's death were already a trial because he was not well and I was all of a sudden thrown in the role of a main caregiver, a mother and teacher to my father. Later, this was almost a blessing, since my daughter was there with me every day helping me take care of him. She saw me feeding him, dressing him, helping him go to the toilet and my husband helping him take a shower. My father refused to go to the hospital so I went to his house at least twice a day for a few hours. In this situation, I began questioning our social structure and family configurations. I was considering having my father move in with us so I could take care of him, and I thought about my husband and me when we grow old. Is my daughter going to be able to take care of us?

Compare it to the old days, when generations lived together, grandparents helped raise children, children and grandchildren helped take care of the elders as they ailed. Coming from a very small and widespread family, I was the only one there to take care of my father. I believe that families are pulling up roots and migrating so much, not realizing we are not only losing the family support, but also the security of being taken care of when we are old. Look at the masses of nursing homes and assisted living complexes. There is a whole industry out there geared and ready to take our old people off of our hands, and take care of them in lieu of being paid. Many of us are not able to take care of our parents for financial, time, and space reasons. We have our own families and hectic lives and being faced with this fact, I was very sad. And what makes it even worse is that this cycle starts when we give our children to a daycare center instead of having family there to help us raise them, and we feel that this is normal.

My husband comes from a family of eight and his parents and grandparents had a lot of children and grandchildren around them to take care of them as they got older. It was never a question if they should be confronted with the sickness or ailments of the elders. Or if any of them would join the funeral services if someone passed away, as children of all ages are continuously faced with death. In our case, people were questioning if my daughter should attend my father's funeral, especially since we had a viewing.

Why is it that most people feel children should not be exposed to this sort of thing? Are we really doing them a favor? Being that my daughter was with me and saw how sick my father was up to the day he passed away, we decided that she should attend the funeral services so that she can have closure. Otherwise, she would always expect Opa to come back. We have always told her that people become angels when they die and that we can always talk to them when we want to. We cannot see them or hug them and sometimes they don't talk back, but they are always around. This is truly my belief, so it is not a fairytale, per say. If you don't believe this way you must really think about how you want to explain the finality of death to your child when it happens. Children need a way to work out seeing a person one day and that person being gone forever the next. Also, skeletons, muscles, and such fascinate my daughter, we let her watch *Forensic Science* and other shows supervised so the thought of a body did not scare her.

All of these things were a blessing when it came time to explain that Opa is dead. It took a few days to sink in and we gave her the option if she wanted to see Opa at his going away celebration. She decided she did and I took a lot of time explaining that Opa would look and feel very different from the last time we saw him. Of course, I never thought about having to explain death to my daughter until it hit me personally. Could I turn back the clock now, I would prepare us all for the situation better. Surely, there are books or movies (Old Yellow?) that are child appropriate that you can use to explain things. Or, by watching nature movies and just explaining how a flower buds, blooms, and dies (a little abstract but it is a good start). You have to be careful not to say, "Because he was old" since you yourself are a fossil in a toddler's eyes! If you use sickness as a reason, your child will panic every time you have a cold, because now you are sick and will die just like so-and-so. Now you see how necessary a plan is.

We explained the situation to her pre-school teacher and sure enough my daughter went to school and told all her friends that her Opa is dead. Some parents expressed their dismay that she scared their children. I had no comment. We encouraged my daughter to speak about her feelings and many days after the funeral service she would talk about it and tell me she missed her Opa. She was digesting the situation and working it out in her own way. Still today she often talks about the last day we spent with him and how she went and gave him an extra hug and kiss...

Some people expected me to hide the fact from my daughter that her Opa was dead, like a loved animal that dies and is secretly replaced. Honestly, can you really replace something you loved? I think death is a part of the life cycle our children need to understand just like birth and growing older. Many other cultures celebrate death giving those that are left behind peace and time to grieve openly.

We often sit outside in our hammock and stare at the night sky, looking for Opa. When we find the brightest blinking star we tell him our feelings and blow Opa a kiss...

EPILOGUE

As this book comes to an end, I hope it has provoked you to laugh, to cry, to think, and to share. I hope it makes you give your children an extra hug and go call your parents.

Most of all, I hope it inspires you to follow your dreams. Sometimes, we need to realize it is time to put our comfort zone to the side and to act on our gut instinct. That nagging feeling in your gut, that is your passion.

Enjoy life, and follow your dreams!

THE END

ABOUT THE AUTHOR

Heike Boehnke-Sharp began her journey as a writer when her daughter was born in 1997. Her upbringing and outstanding women in her life made raising a goddess girl so much easier. Once she discovered that her parenting style had recently been dubbed *attachment parenting* she began writing a column for several online magazines. Coming from a European background her views were often seen as too risky, and her work was censored. Not willing to change the content or message of her articles, Heike decided to launch her own website and GoddessInTheGroove.com was born. She also began writing on issues of multi-cultural families and has been featured in Vegetarian Child, Urbanmozaik.com, GardenPlum.com, & more.

Soon, the Goddess in the Groove became a catalyst for women all around the world. Many talented writers share their work and life experiences here. It has become a community, a place to gather.

The Goddess in the Groove also became the gathering place for Heike's Goddess pendants. Shortly after her daughter's birth, the goddesses began to come to her, each one with a specific mission, or magic, in her belly.

Heike is studying herbal medicine, to complete her "Kitchen Witch" cycle, and fulfill her soul's calling. You can reach her through her website, www.goddessinthegroove.com

www.ingramcontent.com/pod-product-compliance
Lightning Source LLC
Chambersburg PA
CBHW051707040426
42446CB00008B/753